Nothing Left Unsaid; Except Everything After

Amelia DeCoil

BookLeaf Publishing

India | USA | UK

Presentation by *BookLeaf Publishing*

Web: www.bookleafpub.com

E-mail: info@bookleafpub.com

ISBN: 9789360948429

First edition 2024

To the ones I love,

the ones I've lost,

and the ones who have inspired me.

ACKNOWLEDGEMENT

A very special thank you to my twin Amanda, without whom I would have never started writing in the first place. You have and you always will inspire me more than you can ever know.

And of course to my parents Skippy and Sondra who have encouraged me and loved me through it all.

PREFACE

Pieces of every version of myself that I have
been and who I am now.
May this help me hold onto her in every future
me I become.

Unapologetically Myself

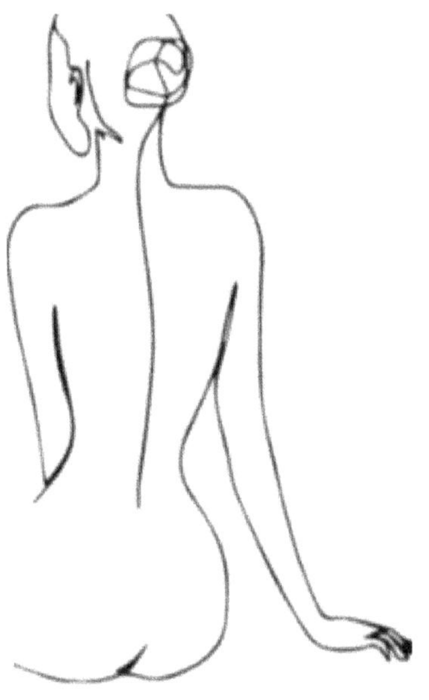

I'll Always Choose Color

When you're strolling through a building and
you notice there's art on the wall

Your first thought isn't why did they hang a
picture up in this hall

Wasn't it beautiful just how it was made

Why did you feel the need to dress it up and
make it this way

When you visit a museum or see street art add
color to places in town

Do you think to yourself the blank walls didn't
need paint, they were beautiful without

Do you question why an artist takes a perfectly
fine blank canvas and brings a picture to life

And tell them after they spent time to make it
just right, 'the solid white canvas was fine'
handing it out for free when they never asked for
your advice

Your body is a temple there's no need to
decorate

Adding body art and makeup means your own
reflection you must hate

Don't you think you're beautiful why do you
feel the need to change

The way you do your makeup is too loud, don't
you know some people will think it's strange

The saying beauty is in the eye of the beholder
may be true

But what about in the mind, don't you know
we're conditioned to ignore that too

Because wearing makeup must only mean one
thing

That I am not happy with the way that I was
made

There are very few things I believe can be
accomplished with a narrow mind

And because that's what society says, does not
mean it's true or that everyone is aligned

To the contrary I feel my natural beauty fits me
to the tee

But that doesn't mean it has to be the only face
for the rest of my life that I see

*
**

I have always admired every form of art

I can close down a museum or spend an entire
day in the park

So when I add blues and pinks and whites and
all the hues of the rainbow to my eyes

This does not mean my natural face I am trying
to hide

÷

Makeup is one of the very few arts I not only
admire but can halfway decently do

And asking if it's because I don't see my own
worth or that my natural beauty is true

Some don't understand why telling me they
think I'm pretty isn't enough to be persuaded

Expected to be defensive as if their opinion is an
interrogation

☐

Yes I so passionately believe in self-love

But why does that definition have to be the one
society pushes onto us and shoves

6

Like everyone I have flaws and there are things I
wish I could change

But that absolutely does not mean I wish I didn't
look this way

It doesn't have to be a choice one or the other

I can think my appearance is beautiful but I can
think the same for colors

I'm not trying to hide my face

I just like living in color and to me makeup is an
art that I love to embrace

Not every genre is understood by all

So if you don't like my bright colors there's
plenty to stare at like a blank wall

Beauty is seen with your eyes

But to appreciate it you first need an open mind

So whether you think I add a spectrum of color
because I don't like the way that I am

Or because I spend a little extra time doing my
makeup, I must be trying to impress a man

I assure you both these theories are the farthest
thing from the truth

I do this for me because in a dark world living in
color will always be the option I choose

Definition: Dictionary vs Society

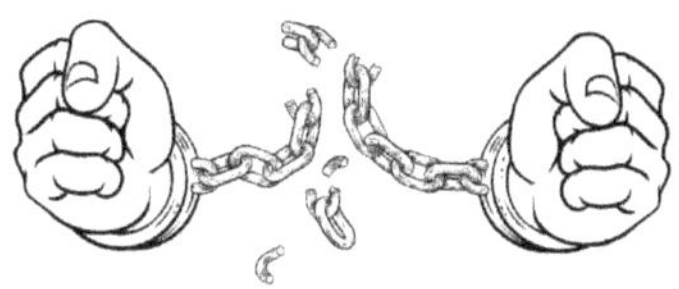

Dictionary definition for I'm sorry

A feeling of sorrow or sympathy

Example given: I'm sorry for your loss

It can be followed by you're in my thoughts

Next definition given is feeling regret

So something like I'm sorry your birthday I always forget

Another way I'm sorry is defined is to be mournful or sad

I'm sorry that for you, today has been bad

And lastly I'm sorry can be said when you're
feeling pitiful

Here could be said something similar to I'm
sorry to someone you love you feel invisible

⌘

I vaguely remember learning random definitions
in school

There's the textbook kind but the one we all
seem to remember is the definitions given by
society, like what it means to be cool

I can't quite tell you at what age societal
standards were instilled in us like memorizing
the study questions for our life's exam

Society telling us everything we need to be in
that very first glance

So many detrimental expectations being forced
on to us before we were even old enough to
realize

Till you're molded into someone who benefits
their reality some don't even remember who they
were before they became their disguise

We each hold onto the definition society created for us, for some the biggest parts are different and for some the same

At the end of the day the action of being molded provides the same outcome but sometimes called a different name

So for me maybe it's not the biggest standard thrown on to me but probably the one I hate the most

Is all the reasons to say I'm sorry, ever since I can remember that's the best way to do what I'm told

So let's break down what that looks like this day in age

Because the older I get the more I realize that apologizing for the sake of it is the shackles in society's cage

⌘

Being in a corporate career I assure you it's no myth that every time I'm in a meeting outnumbered by men

They jump in and cut each other off, never once
is an apology given

But any time a woman jumps in the conversation
I'm sorry is said at least in the beginning and end
and usually a few more times because that's the
expectation

It took me so long to realize I too apologize
more than I should, not because I am sorry but
because it felt like an obligation

Sometimes when I'm working out in the gym
and I talk when I have my headphones on I feel
the need to apologize for being too loud

Too loud in a place with music blaring, weights
dropping, people grunting, yet I'm sorry for
being a tiny sound lost in the crowd

Or even when a person talks over me my first
reaction is to say I'm sorry, you go ahead

But to be honest I'm not sorry and quite frankly
apologizing is actually what I regret

If I counted every second I spent saying I'm
sorry when it wasn't true

I wonder just how long I've spent not being
honest because society made me feel like that's
what I should do

How many minutes and days and months and
years I've lessened myself because of society's
expectation

Diminishing my voice out of the duty to some
made-up obligation

⌘

So now I actively choose to be unapologetic as
fuck when it comes to situations I should be
sorry according to society

I will no longer apologize for being who I am
because I was not meant to live quietly

I will never truly feel sorry for taking up space

Or for removing my disguise and showing my
true face

When I have a thought or contribution to give to
a conversation

I will not apologize, I'm breaking the chains of
that obligation

My thoughts my opinions and who I am as a
person, no matter what I'll tell my story

And I will only say it when it's following the
true definition, other than that, **no I am not
sorry**

1000 Days Sober

There was a time I couldn't even fathom being where I am

Never in a million years would this have ever been my plan

As long as I kept going back to the bottom of a bottle

I thought I could forget all my problems and struggles

When you spend your nights dancing with the devil

You can convince yourself the flames are just
superficial

Always saying I could stop when I wanted to

Never knowing who I was trying to convince
that that was true

Waking every morning with more than regret

Still every night I played Russian roulette with
life and death

Spiraling down the gates of hell he led me to the
lowest levels

Swaying back and forth too faded to realize I
was dancing with the devil

For years I held on to the excuse that I needed
alcohol to be fun

I never remembered when my demons were in
control and who they made me become

It took so long to see the irony of the bottle
being a double-edged sword

Running from my demons when I was sober
only for the alcohol to intensify them more

The nightly blackouts drowned out that I knew I
needed help

Waiting for somebody or anyone really, but
when a bottle was involved, not even I could
save me from myself

From the outside I knew how to make it seem
like I was living out my dreams

But behind closed doors my alcohol addiction
was tearing me apart at the seams

When I was sober I believed the delusion that it
could fix the parts of me that were broken

Only for it to pull me under and cause so much
more destruction

Looking back now I truly have no idea how I
survived

So many nights that I should have never made it
out alive

It took losing everything I was and hurting all
the ones I loved

So many tears shed and my hands covered in
blood

When I was at my lowest I knew I had to look
within

And then I had to decide if I wanted my life to
begin or end

I decided I would do whatever it would take to
break out of my addiction I was shackled to

I broke all the bottles that held me prisoner as a
victim to my own torture and abuse

I had to break free from my delusional reality
that I believed in for so long

Be truthful with myself about how I could be
alright once I accepted that everything was so
wrong

1000 days ago I made the one-second decision
to give myself a fighting chance to become the
person I wanted to be

The hardest part was knowing the things I did
and accepting them as who I was so I could
finally truly be free

It took one unwavering commitment to myself in
a matter of moments

After years of denial I faced the reality of my
addiction and knew its cycle had to be broken

I've faced my demons and asked them for their
name

They answered with shame and pointed all their
fingers everywhere else to assign the blame

I showed them a mirror and started calling them
with acceptance and showed them love

I told them even with scars so deep and regrets
so loud, we may be broken but we can still be
enough

After all this time on the journey of recovery,
now that I'm on the other side of my addiction

In some ways I'm still broken and still struggle
but I'm no longer in the confines of that liquid
prison

I've taken back control of my own life

And even during my worst days, I know I'm
going to be alright

After 1000 days of choosing myself and fighting
to let go of the demons that haunted me for all
those years

The chains of addiction will never again hold me
captive in fear

Aquarius Arrow

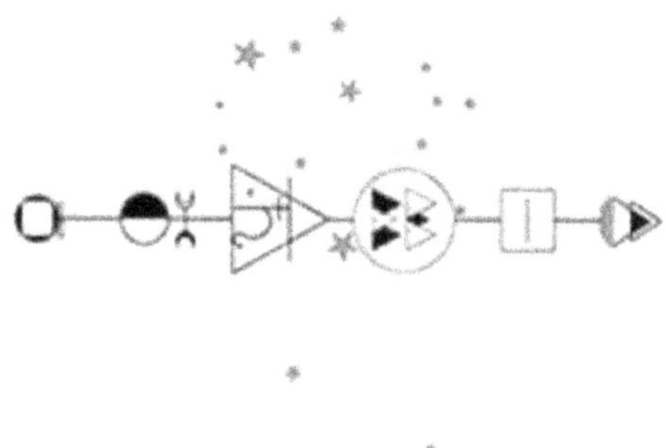

I'm an Aquarius but let me tell you what that
means to me

Because there's a lot that most people who don't
know wouldn't believe

Aquarius is a fixed sign

So I hold on to ideas and my own sense of right
and wrong never leave my mind

When there's something I want or believe in, it
takes a lot for me to let it go

So what I spend my energy on is always true and
just and may take effort beyond what is seen as
possible but I'll achieve it, from the beginning
this I already know

If it's not achievable or something I truly care
about I don't waste a single second thought on it

Because when I focus or start something until I
have succeeded I will not quit

Some dreams I've had and spent time working
on and obsessing over with tunnel vision seem
to be far bigger than may seem possible to others

In the end my determination and unconventional
mentality bring me success with each new dream
and goal of mine that I discover

To others it may seem like my luck is endless
but I assure you that's never been the case

Behind closed doors my success is only
achieved by my hard work and determination
that each time I embrace

☐

As an Air Sign I know I often seem uninterested
and aloof

But beyond my natural RBF I can assure you
that at least some of the time that isn't actually
true

Fill my time with intellect and curiosity and the
true aspect of what is right and wrong

And my interest and focus will be yours all day
long

But small talk, gossip, and society's standards
and expectations will be the fastest way for me
not to bother myself with a single word you say

Because small-minded viewpoints will only
annoy me and make me ignore you in every way

So although my face and voice are monotone to
the point I've gotten used to saying out loud
when I'm excited or happy

If I spend energy in a discussion no matter how
uninterested it may seem I am, I don't waste my
words so judge my interest by that because that's
the only way I'll ever be chatty

In true Aquarius fashion we are ruled by two
completely opposite ruling planets Uranus and
Saturn

The two couldn't be more different in their
influential patterns

Saturn holds great influence focusing on
structure and leadership

But it's preferred to have an unofficial form in a
natural way because anything more than that
will feel fake because it will never come from
anything seeming like an ego trip

I feel most satisfied encouraging others because
to my core I believe when one person succeeds
in a meaningful way we all do

So I spend my time showing and telling others
what they're capable of because sometimes they
just need to be reminded of how much they can
achieve if they already believe it's true

Uranus on the other hand has a strong influence
on rebellion and freedom

And my need for freedom is always the
backbone to everything I do and everything I
focus on leads straight to that very reason

But the rebellion of an Aquarius is not rooted in
evil or mayhem

More so in what society may not see as things
worth saving

Due to believing so deeply in our own personal
definition of right and wrong

Regardless of the common viewpoint of others,
we will fight for what we believe in even if we
have to fight alone

As an Aquarius I embrace the life of a
homebody

Because I feel at home with my own thoughts
than with random people's company

So it's easy to overlook just how important
social aspects are to me

Because it's key to know what is important is
rarely an individual but more so all of humanity

In my very core I believe all living souls; people
and animals alike are those of equal

And that anything less is the fastest way to
achieve a life opposite of peaceful

We are so deeply rooted and passionate about
improving the social well-being of all
humankind

The world will only truly be at its potential when
that concept and the opportunity for all actually
align

The other focus of that is with the animal
kingdom and their ability to live out their
longest possible life

It will never be okay for humans to decide how
long they get to be alive

And lastly and not at all the least important is
the well-being of mother nature and her chance
to thrive

For it is true when humans choose their greed
and kill her it's very easy to see that without
mother nature us humans cannot survive

These truths are the ones that will always be the
backbone of everything I believe in

Because we will all lose when the voiceless
cannot win

As an Aquarius I fully embrace my
unconventional ideology in every way

Always ready for the next place to move
because I very rarely feel I fit in making it so
easy not to stay

While to some this may seem sad or lonely but
to me I find peace, happiness, and comfort in my
solitude

And my thoughts and opinions on how to
continue forward progress I know can bring
inspiration as my unusual way of thinking can
provide a different view

So although the thought of never fitting in may
be a scary thought for some

To me it only provides so many endless
possibilities to create the person I want to
become

I will never understand or believe the best way
forward is based on tradition

Because if history has shown us anything it's
that when it comes to mother nature, human, and
animal life that mindset has only caused division

So when you think you know what I'm feeling or
thinking I can almost always assure you you're
wrong

Because in true Aquarius fashion I am far more
than meets the eye, this I've known for so very
long

But if there's anything that's obvious about me
it's that if I give you my time or attention it's
never out of habit or force

Because the energy and time I give to others is
always and intentionally scarce

So to those that hold my attention just know to
me you're in high regard

Because those I feel safe within all the
unconventional ways, around you it's easy to let
down my guard

Imprints of Grief

Grief

I was five years old when grief first introduced
itself to me

Back then I was too young to fully understand
that once he comes he never leaves

I didn't quite understand that our last words were
spoken to each other and our love and laughter
would only ever remain in what has been

You weren't just my grandpa you were my hero,
the greatest man to ever live, my best friend

I didn't know that every holiday after would feel
so hollow

Or that when I begged to go see you that last
time, after that I would always and forever hate
hospitals

I hadn't yet learned how painful it would be to
dream of sitting on your back porch listening to
the rain create music on your tin roof

That the only thing I'd ever be able to hold on to
was your memory and knowing that in those five
short years your love trapped in time would be
my light and even after all these years I still feel
the bittersweetness of that truth

You were bigger than the whole sky

And I couldn't comprehend it then but there's
nothing that broke me more than kissing you on
the cheek for the last time and saying goodbye

Even now as an adult every day I still miss you

My tiny child heart loved you more than
anything I ever knew

∾

I remember driving from Florida to Virginia one
winter all those years ago

A winter of firsts, meeting you and seeing snow

I remember getting out of the car and meeting
you for the first time

Your cutoff sleeves and big burly beard, I was so
shy

It didn't take long to warm up to you, you were
just a teddy bear underneath your grizzly voice
and tattoos

I remember standing in the kitchen listening to
you whistle telling me it's the best thing to do
when you're feeling blue

Man your laughter felt like it would carry on for
days

When our vacation was over I still wanted to
stay

Fast forward a few years to spending the
summer with you when we were in high school

No longer shy, your tattoos and long burly beard
now made you seem even more cool

I remember the time you fell asleep so we
braided your beard in pigtails

It's like that summer I remember every detail

One night we came home from work to see you
sleeping on the couch with the dogs cuddled all
around a beer in your hand and on the tv was
Finding Nemo

Gawd how I miss you so much Uncle Leebo

Or that time we drove out to New York City for
twenty-four hours and people kept asking us to
stop

Every time they asked for your autograph cause
they thought you were in ZZ Top

Waking up to the smell of fresh homemade
donuts you spent all morning making

And on your birthday I spent the day in my
room sneaking ingredients in so I could surprise
you with a cake but the oven in the kitchen it
turns out is key when you're baking

So you made up some errands you needed to run

Cause even though you already knew what I was doing you didn't want to ruin the fun

That summer was one for the books that I will forever cherish in my memory

And to this day every now and then I can still feel your energy

I remember hearing about the cancer and how fast it was spreading

Knowing grief would once again bring back the feelings that I was dreading

The next summer I spent in Virginia after you were gone

On your birthday I walked across the street sat by your grave drinking beers and watching a meteor shower all night long

Once again you lit up my world like you always seemed to do

And I'll spend the rest of my life not wishing on shooting stars but asking them to make their way to you and tell you just how much I miss and love you

I remember the summers spent with you and all
the laughs we shared

Running through the yard wind blowing in my
long blonde hair

There's no one I loved quite like you

They say not to pick favorites but out of all my
cousins you were the coolest one I knew

I remember seeing you in the hospital when our
world stopped and we didn't know if you would
live

My adolescent heart couldn't bear to learn again
the pain that grief would once again give

So when you got better and recovered from your
overdose I knew I never wanted to ever let you
go

You were both lightning and thunder but also the
most beautiful rainbow

We had twenty-three extraordinary years full of
love laughter and your spitfire remarks

You lit the whole world on fire you were so
much bigger than a spark

All those times I called and you would say just
how proud of me you were

Planning out our future, we were cousins but we
were best friends first

Then the one night I didn't answer your call

Saying I'd call you back tomorrow, I had no idea
I was wrong

If I would have answered your very last call that
Thanksgiving night

Would you still be here would the world be
alright

I'll never know the answers to the questions
about that night I lost so much

I'll never again be able to tell you I love you give
you a hug and feel your touch

After the world grew dark you haunted me in my dreams

Only to wake up to your name I would scream

For months and months my dreams told me I could have saved you

All I needed to do was answer the phone but now my biggest regret in life was something I didn't do

Now all I have are the memories of when you made my whole world brighter

A video of when you surprised me for my college graduation, gawd I wish I would've hugged you tighter

Adventures in Tennessee and the days spent floating on the Shenandoah River

Funny how those memories now seem so much bigger

There's not a single day that goes by I don't question how or why we had to say goodbye

But I know always and forever I will love you
for my whole life

❧

Going to a small high school meant everyone
knew everyone

Every friend I had was different but none
compared to you, each one a star but you were
the sun

We were so young just trying to learn who we
were

Looking back our memories so clear but the
years are such a blur

We were there for each other back when we
thought we loved shitty dudes

I don't remember them well but I know I'll never
forget you

You taught me so much about life in those few
short years

Through the love, laughter, learning, and tears

Spending so many nights at your house with
face masks and crazy pictures

You were more than a best friend, you were my
sister

I remember one day you told me that
'soulmates' wasn't just for lovers

It's anyone that you would love for the rest of
your forever

So we saved each other in our phones and in our
memories as just that, soulmates

And even though life continued on and we grew
apart, to me that's how you forever stayed

I reached out a few times over the years

Always thinking I'd be able to again but now I
only talk to you through the tears

Although our lives went separate ways

There are so many things I wish I could say

Like how proud I was of the life you chose for
so long

Being sober in this world can sometimes make
you feel weak even when you're so strong

You held on so long and was an inspiration to so
many

Then all it took was one night, and now the
heartbreak is so heavy

I'll never forget the night I found out, how empty
I felt

It truly didn't seem fair, the cards you were dealt

Once again the memories are all I have left to
hold onto

Freeze frames in my mind of perfect moments I
shared with you

For the rest of my days I know you'll be the first
person I remember when I think about soulmates
and best friends

And no matter how much time goes on I'll
always love you till the very end

Grief steals so much of who you are

It takes beautiful memories and turns them into
painful scars

It takes the tears you once cried from laughing
so much

And turns them to endless soul-wrenching tears
cause you know you'll never again feel their
touch

I'm not a lover of many but those I've loved I
have done so with every part of my being

And each time their forever goodbye comes life
always seems to lose its meaning

The good, the bad, the beautiful, and the sad of
moments with the ones I'll forever treasure

Knowing that there were once perfect moments
in time because we were together

Over the years grief shows up so sporadic and
sometimes right on cue

I can feel it consume me because I listened to a
song that reminded me of you

Or be swallowed up by the grip of grief for no
reason at all

Other than the fact after all this time each of you
I wish I could still call

When I feel the heartbreak of the missing pieces
of my heart

I don't numb it or get mad or ask for it to part

I sit with the bittersweet memories of what used
to be

And I send each one of you my love wherever
you may be

Please know you'll never just be a single
memory

For every second I was lucky to love you has
made me shackled to heartbreak but in your
love, forever free

Your Love Will Live On

As I stand here today I'm still in disbelief

There's no way to truly and profoundly comprehend grief

But in this room here, I know we all share something more consuming than our hearts so deeply filled with sorrow

I know, even more than that, we will always love you and carry you into every single one of our tomorrows

Your heart was so full and your soul so beautifully untamed

Although, no matter how hard we try, it's so
difficult not to mix grief together with blame

What if I would have…? Why didn't I…? Would
a check-in message have saved her…? Would
everything be different now…?

These questions to ourselves can be asked a
million different ways and each one seems to
progressively get more loud

But if we just stop for a moment and listen
instead to the whisper

We can hear the love you gave to all of us, and
during the difficult time ahead it will become
like a lullaby of a cascading river

.

You were a light in this world so vibrant and
beautiful with a laugh that will forever echo in
every one of our souls

You had a way of showing us that when life
turns people into roses their petals are beautiful
but so are their thorns

You were always so raw and authentic knowing
that as humans our complexities are not only
made up of just the negatives or just the
positives

That it's not that simplistic because what makes
us who we are is so much more ambiguous

We all have both angels and demons we collect
over the years

They blur the lines and use empty promises to
disguise instead what we should fear

At its very core addiction is a disease with no
regard for the person it has claimed as its own,
and takes everything it can

It has so many ways to trick you whispering lies
as it drags you down the gates of hell while
convincing you what it's offering is peace and a
helpful hand

The second-hand smoke from this relentless
disease fills the lungs and souls of all those
around with unbearable sorrow and heartbreak

And leaves our world in devastation like the
aftermath of a destructive earthquake

As we pick up the rubble we use your memories
and love you shared with us to slowly put the
pieces of our shattered hearts back together

No matter how much time passes by we'll carry
the stitches of your love in our hearts and the
memories of your laughter and smile will be
with us forever

.

No matter how you became so lucky to have had
her intertwined in your life, I have no doubt she
showed you so much love

Whether it was a moment in time or years that
seemed to have gone by in the blink of an eye,
either way it will now never seem long enough

We'll hold on to your memories that are etched
in our minds

What you meant to us and the very person we
are so directly aligned

For there is not a single soul you connected with
and did not change their life

For your soul was so beautiful and you were so
generous with your glowing light

.

I don't know if this goodbye will ever seem real

The heart shattered by grief leaves more than
just scars, I don't know if they can ever truly
heal

There are so many things that get left unsaid
when a life gets taken so early by death, the
worst of thieves

But I know for the rest of all of our lives we'll
see you again in our dreams

You'll forever be in our hearts because to know
you was to love you from the very beginning

To have known you is to love you because even
without you in this world your love will never
stop living

9/11

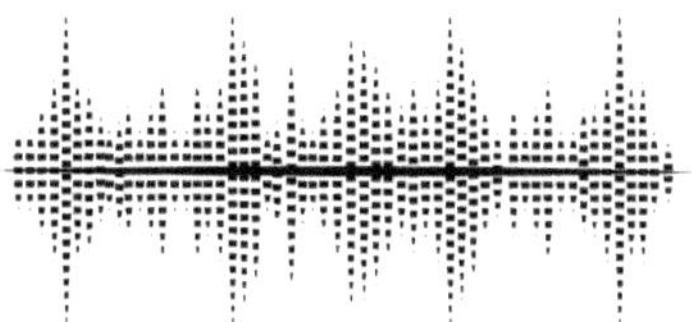

America will always remember this day

It touched our hearts in every way

All those years ago when the pentagon was hit and the twin towers fell

Our world screamed out like a horrifying bell

Husband, children and wives

All lost their lives

Their silence is louder than any sound

You can still hear their cries from when the buildings hit the ground

This day is a reminder why we fight to be free

So our kids won't have to see what we had to see

We'll always remember the heroes that fell

And the ones still alive with a story to tell

Dearly Beloved

Twinship

To the ones who ask what's it like being a twin
because they genuinely want to know

I often respond what is it like to not be a twin,
but now I'll answer your question in a flow

We came into this world already having seven
and a half months together

And the thirty years since, man they've been an
adventure

Before we pieced together our first words that
others could understand

Our hearts spoke to each other, always hand in
hand

Our twin telepathy has always been activated

And may just be one of the ways of our bond
and sometimes feels so understated

One of us crying and screaming at the top of our
lungs

Our parents frantically trying to figure out what
was wrong only to figure it out when they
checked on the quiet one

So many crazy stories from times we don't
remember just how in sync we've always been

Before we were born and since we have been
lucky enough to know that being a twin is
beyond sisters and best friends

We are truly one soul in two bodies

One heart made in two copies

No words need to be spoken, our love will
always be my favorite sound

Although just like everyone else we have our
ups and downs

But on the days we drive each other crazy

Our love still never fades or becomes hazy

We inspire each other to always become better

Knowing no matter what our love will be
forever

We can tell each other the hard things even when
it's difficult to hear

Because we know even on our worst days each
other's hand will always be near

Growing up we went through the different
phases, always wanting to be together and
wanting to be our own person

But the love we had for one another never once
took a diversion

After being together every day for eighteen
years we learned what it meant to be apart

The early part of our adult years we truly learned
no matter how far away we were, we still carried
each other in our own hearts

And even though the only way we could see
each other was through FaceTime

Our twinning, thus far was actually in its prime

More times than not we'd see each other on the
screen and both be wearing the same clothes

Our minds have always been so alike but our
bond became even stronger when we spent time
finding each other's individuality, stepping out of
one another's shadows

We spent a decade both finding who we were on
our own

Different cities, states, and countries but we
always knew we were never actually alone

It's been two years since we added roommates to
our twinship description

Seeing each other grow and bloom always one
another's inspiration

Having been apart allowed us to truly appreciate the beauty of how lucky we are to be twins

I don't know why but I'll be forever grateful the universe allowed us to have a bond stronger than sisters and best friends

We might not have it all figured out

But with you by my side this life is so beautiful that I'll never doubt

Because even on our worst days, biggest heartbreaks, or when life gets dark and we can't find the light

All we have to do is look towards each other to know our love will always make everything alright

So thank you for being so much more than a sister and a best friend

I know forever and always your love will make me the luckiest because you're my twin

Neither one of us will ever truly be alone this we understand

Because we have and always will go through life
hand in hand

In the silence or during the loudest times we will
love each other beyond what could be described

Because we have each other forever and always
we'll know love for the rest of our lives

My Grumpy Old Man Dog Best Friend

They say dogs are a woman's best friend

But those words don't seem encompassing
enough to explain just how much I'll love Colby
till the very end

You see Colby was born specifically to be my
dog

Even on my worst days my love for him is so
very strong

I remember waking up one day when I was in
college feeling like something was missing from
my life

Growing up with dogs I knew just how much
their love can take your darkest days and make
them bright

So after going to a few different shelters I
walked into the kennel room and all the way in
the back I fell in love the first time our eyes met

I knew forever till the end of time we would be
the best of friends

Although he only weighed forty pounds with the
long body and short legs of a Basset Hound

His face is that of a pit bull so in the loudest
room with the biggest dogs, that's where he was
found

I didn't even have to meet him before I told the
lady that he was the one

Looking into his eyes it felt as if I've already
loved him for so long

So I paid twenty dollars for the best friend I'll
have ever

They said that I was his third adoption so if I
brought him back he would be euthanized in the
shelter

Their words fell on deaf ears because I knew
that Colby was not just going to be my dog and
best friend but also my soulmate

It's been eight years since the day our lives
changed and we met our fate

It was very apparent he had some puppyhood
trauma

But since I clicked his leash that first time he
knew I would forever and always be his momma

Ever since our beautiful and special bond
formed it was easy to see we were both so much
alike

Neither one of us really people fans; he's happy
to give me an excuse for "I'm sorry, I can't
come out tonight"

He's been with me through so many of life's
different phases

No matter where we were always excited for me
to get home and welcome me back with his
warm embraces

We've shared nine different houses together and
filled each one with so much love for one
another

A few guys I dated that he met but I knew if
Colby didn't like them they would never be my
lover

He's got a growl that makes him seem like he's a
hundred pounds

He'd protect me with his life I have no doubt

I've been asked if he's mean because he's a
Pitbull so I say he's not mean he just doesn't like
you

Because he's my protector and that will always
be true

I really believe he's me in dog form with his
short little legs and muscles for days

His favorite is being lazy and enjoys a good
cuddle puddle, always

Through all this time and all the things we've
been through together

I rescued him but so many times he's saved me,
always making my life better

He truly was born and put on this earth just to be
my dog, this I know

I've loved him yesterday today and always will
for every one of my tomorrows

Because he's my grumpy old man dog best
friend

And forever and always we'll love each other till
the very end

Big Brothers Big Sisters

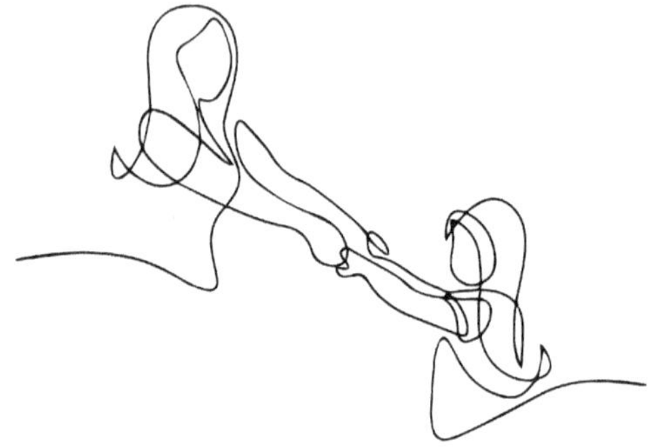

Throughout my whole life I've never wanted kids of my own

Although society says you should, that's not the only way to go

But mentoring and caring for the younger generations has always been important to me

Because I remember how fast I lost hope when I was younger that you could be anyone or anything I wanted to be

Everyone has at least one thing that makes their childhood hard

This world has a cruel way to convince you that you can never get far

Every chance that I can I will shout it from the
rooftops to just keep fighting to be everything
you ever wanted

And that everyone is loved by someone because
that's something kids need reminded of to be
honest

So I applied to be a Big Sister; an interview,
background check, some trainings and a few
months later I had no idea how much my life
was about to change

You see I applied hoping to mentor, love, and
give hope to someone younger than me but now
looking back I had no idea how much I would
truly gain

I read somewhere that children don't need to
learn to be happy because they already know

But adults put happiness on the back burner and
hold onto society's expectations and standards,
making the concept of 'happy' easy to let go

This she showed me on the first outing we did
together

When our original plans fell through she showed
me that happiness comes even from the little
pleasures

As I was frantically scrolling through my phone
to try to figure out something cool we could do

She gasped really loud and asked if I liked
animals and when I said of course her smile
instantly grew

She searched in my phone maps and within
seconds handed it back to me with a route
already started

Nervous cause I was the typical broke adult,
when I looked at the destination I was a little
confused but from the ice cream shop we
departed

When we walked into the pet store I was still
apprehensive as I didn't think her parents would
appreciate me dropping her off at home with a
new pet

Skipping through the doors this is going to be so
fun she said

Then she grabbed my hand and said nothing
better than playing with all the animals here

We asked an employee if we could hold the
hamsters and guinea pigs and talked to the birds
and watched the cats play that were near

After a while of both of us having fun with
smiles on our faces I took her home and hugged
her so tight before I left

Two years later and that day I know I will never
forget

Ever since, we've hung out at least a couple
times a month

And every time is full of happiness, life talks,
and so much love

Big Brothers Big Sisters always giving us the
coolest opportunities

Like going to watch the Bucs games during
playoffs right by the field for free

We've gone to an animal farm, had a Top Golf
takeover, learned tennis, toured a private airline

hanger with a photoshoot in private planes, and
got skateboard lessons with Boards for Bros

From sports to holiday celebrations to all
different kinds of shows

I could fill a whole page with all the cool stuff
we've done

But every time looking back through all the
events and laughter and being there when she
just needed to cry, both of our hearts have grown
with so much love

Out of all of the matches in the counties in our
area we were one of a few chosen to do an
interview for the sixtieth anniversary celebration

We walked in with cameras and sound systems
and a crew who put on our mics and told her not
to be nervous we were just going to have a fun
conversation

It was beautiful that once she got past the nerves
man did she blossom and show everyone there
her fun bubbly personality

She told them she wanted to go to college in
Africa but it's fine because we'd always be best
friends and man did my heart melt instantly

A few years ago when I decided to move here I
had no rhyme or reason why this place was the
only one on my list

I had no friends here and my family still lives far
away but this is where I had to be I'd insist

Looking back now I know it was so we could be
in each other's lives

Our fates came together like the most beautiful
design

Before we got matched I was so excited to
impact the younger generations, it meant so
much to me

But two years later I now know that she's
impacted my life even more, now that's so easy
to see

As life has a knack of being a rollercoaster we
now and always will have each other to talk to
and have a comforting hand to hold

As we both get older we have taken turns giving
each other hope

Growing up in this world can be so very difficult
to do

So as much as I can I remind her I'm always
there for her no matter what she's going through

And although she's twenty years younger than
me you would never know

She reminds me no matter what part of the
rollercoaster of life I'm going through that
happiness and laughter can always be found at
the pet store and we can always go

Seasons of Lovers

I'm a firm believer that people show up in your
life at the exact moment they should

And they leave for a reason even if the reason is
not understood

I have loved another for what felt like a lifetime

And others our passion only lasted a fortnight

But regardless of the length of time spent, every
time it was always magical

Some lovers I spent every second with while
some lived in other countries, because love
never pays mind to what others see as
impractical

Each time I grew and learned and morphed into
another version of me

All of these versions I know they are who I was
supposed to be

Through happiness and heartbreak; in between
the hello and goodbye

As I grow older I now no longer see the need to
ask why

Because I know every person I've loved I've
loved for a reason

Each person I've loved throughout my life each
one defining a different season

Who I am and who I'm with just like fingerprints
in time, special in their own way

But each one I've loved differently, teaching me
that it's okay to change

So I live in the happiness and I allow the sadness
when it ends

Because each one shows me a new piece of my
heart, it's easy to see the trend

So thank you to the few who brought out the
lover in me

It's a side of myself I guard and only let a few
see

So no matter what phase or how long I keep it
locked up, I'm grateful for every lover I meet

For I am who I am because of the ones who have
set my love free

Two Souls

Two souls together in a moment in time

With eyeS closed bodies intertwined

Clutching skin And clutching breaths

In this Moment there's only beginnings, nothing ends

♡

Two souls lost in a momEnt in time

Hand in hand floating by the dead sea shoReline

Smiles on our faces and our hearts

You were so beautiful to me from the start

I study your features every chance that I could

Knowing our time will come to an end I so
reluctantly understood

♡

Two beautiful souls become one just for a
moment in time

Even though things are complicated it felt so
alluring for you to be mine

All things come to an end so we said goodbye

But with you every enchanting moment was
worth the tears that I cried

I would choose our moments in time over and
over again

Because we were magic even though we both
knew it would end

♡

Two lonely souls walking this earth

But finding a soul that brought out mine, to me
the price it was worth

So I wiped my tears and dropped your hand

And I'll wait for the days I can pick it up again

♡

Two wondrous souls counting down the days

When between us there's no more space

We'll explore all the beauty this world has to
show

We'll love the moment and know it's worth the
goodbye that's just how it goes

♡

Two longing souls on two different roads

But when they come together the infatuation
leaves us at a crossroads

But I wouldn't trade a single second no matter
how sad the goodbye is

Because when my soul speaks to yours I know
how beautiful that is

Shall We Dance

You're as beautiful as the stars in the night sky

As gentle as the clouds floating by

Your laugh is as euphoric as the melody to all my favorite songs

Your heartbeat is the tune that makes me feel at home

When your soul speaks to mine it's like the perfect dance

Not a second goes by that I don't wish I was holding your hand

The way we sway back and forth in perfect
tempo

The happiness we feel is from our hearts, the
most beautiful echo

When all the music ends and the world grows
quiet

The beat of your heart sings to mine and leaves
me inspired

Inspired to be more than I already am

Knowing now I have you and together
throughout the days we will dance

Each other's happiness is the song that's stuck in
our brains

Regardless of all the miles that separate still we
dance again and again

Your words carry the weight of the world

You make me want to spin around and twirl

I'm confident by myself but baby you make me feel so pretty

I'd dance with you all night long till I'm dizzy

So take my hand and listen to the song of my heart

Even still it sings for you across all the miles that we're apart

This dance we've been doing is as beautiful as can be

So close your eyes take my hand and dance with me

The beat of your heart is etched in my mind

And I'll hear it in my dreams till we're dancing together side by side

Romance

Baby be mine

BecauSe I'd choose you every single night

Your heArtbeat is the only melody I want to fall asleep to

Let this path and every obstacle prove even though we live in different countries destiny had its reasons for me to Meet you

The fingErtips I wanna know are on the end of your hands

Baby show me Romance

.

I'll meet you halfway around the world

If you promise to kiss me and let me be your girl

In the morning when I open mine let me be
looking into your eyes

Breath your breath into me, baby make me feel
alive

You and I are a once in a lifetime chance

Baby show me romance

.

Grab my hand as we once again catch a flight

Every adventure we've already had has been the
time of my life

Making beautiful memories in magical places

With you by my side everything is better no
matter the complications

I wanted you since that very first glance

Baby show me romance

.

Nothing in the world makes sense unless you're
mine

I'm the moon baby you're my sunshine

We follow each other all around this earth

And during the times together our two souls
become one as our hearts merge

We're written in the stars, not just a circumstance

Baby show me romance

.

We'll count down the days till we're once again
hand in hand

Until then every night we'll meet in our
dreamland

We'll explore the beauty down the unbeaten path

Even though we're so far away I know you and I
can last

So be my partner in life's dance

Baby show me romance

Dual Temptation

As I run my fingertips Across your velvet
exterior and breathe in your heavenly aroma

Teasing each other with such a lustful persoNa

A feverish shiver creaTes an eminent vibration
between our flesh

Transcending our clasHing worlds, bribing all
consciousness to a rest

.

Awakening Our sleeping souls

Neither oNe of us can maintain control

As we start to dance around our contagioslY
covetous desires

Gripping the breathlessness of each other,
bringing our skeletons back to life like a blazing
fire

.

Dancing around the dimming lights

Taking each other to new heights

Our bodies keeping beat with the melody of our
concomitant breathing

clutching each other simultaneously so freeing

.

As long as we're in this lustful state of feeling
alive

With one another's breath, each other we revive

My mouse like character daunts the diminishing
elephant that's crowding the room

As whom we have become to each other
ravishingly blooms

All while our shadows create an electrifying
puppet show along the Crimson wall

Back and forth, together we crawl

.

Bodies dripping with heated passion

Dramatically accelerating our lustful chain
reaction

High from the phenylethylamine that we have
become for each other

Our passion as riveting as midnight thunder

Only to wake up with the chemistry of our
paradoxical emotions

Coming down from an all-consuming love
potion

Ignoring the burden of our postulating souls

Feeling everything deep down to our very bones

Memories on a Bike

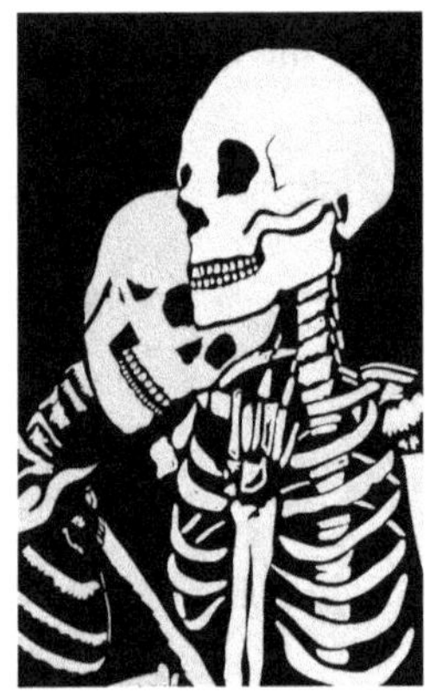

BAck in a previous time

I looked iNto his eyes and everything just felt right

It felT as if I've known him longer than I've known myself

THe first time we met felt like waking up from a spell

After that mOment the world only felt right when I woke up by his side

ChasiNg the sunsets every night riding on the back of his bike

Hearing the sound of the waves lullabY us to sleep

Tangled in each other's arms in a house still being built down on the beach

Going together to other worlds in our minds

Laying on a blanket in the grass lost in our third eye

Before my first time abroad we spent hours eating at an all you can eat sushi buffet

Looking back now that moment I wish I could always have stayed

The midnight calls across time zones felt like home

I thought, him, I would always know

But now the only glimpse of him I see

Is in the faces of strangers every now and again I pass on the street

Every once in a while I think of who we use
to be, him and I

And I smile because we truly were meant to
be, but that was in another life

I wonder if I saw him again

Would our souls talk or would we just be
acquaintances

Back when life only began when I looked
into his eyes

When in the first moment I knew in a
previous life, he was mine

Now the details are blurry but still to this day
I relive them in my dreams

And after all these years the only thing that
makes sense is that he was the love of my
life, it seems

But now his eyes are just a distant memory I
rarely let myself indulge

Thinking how I felt for him, coming alive,
living on impulse

Back then it felt like we had the world in the
palm of our hands

Always remembering, I knew our entire
story in our very first glance

So I hope we meet again in our next life and
every one after

Maybe in one of them we'll forever find
comfort in each other's laughter

But until then I'll remember you when
strangers subtly remind me of who we used
to be

Once upon a time when I loved you and you
loved me

Different Days

Some days happineSs is as beautiful as the blue
that shimmered from the dead sea

Some dAys the most magical thing in this world
is you and me

SoMe days the sun that brightens up my life is
reflected by your perfect smile

SomE days we have nothing but time to sit and
talk and laugh for a while

Some days the bReeze that feels so good is your
breath on the other side of our call

And some days I feel so close to you like it's
safe for me to fall

But some days the sky turns gray

And those days I wonder how long you'll want
to stay

Some days the thunder gets so loud it makes my
tear ducts shake

Some days I can't fight my tears and tell them to
go away

Some days the rain falls from my eyes like
they're clouds in the sky

And some days the storm feels almost familiar
and unfairly await for your goodbye

Some days the gloom feels like it's suffocating
the happiness that we have created

Some days I feel that my storm erases your
happiness and all that's left is your right to be
frustrated

Some days the lightning crashes and I fear the
aftermath will be too much damage

And some days I don't like my own insecurities
so I wait for you to say I'm too much for you to
manage

❧

Some days are bad even when a lot of days are
perfect

Some days are both but our happiness it doesn't
affect

Some days just knowing we have each other the
weather doesn't even matter

And some days regardless of storms or sunshine
all I hear is the lullaby of your laughter

Some days I feel content as we weather the
storm

But on all days there's one thing I always know
for sure

❧

On all days I know I'd rather face a million
storms with you than a single day without you

Every day no matter how loud the thunder is in
my thoughts my heart wants you, it's true

Every day no matter what is better with you than
without

The hard days are better with you, this I truly
never doubt

Some days I don't feel I deserve to ask you for
anything

And those days I ask anyway to just tell me it
will all be okay, I hope that's not strange

Every day I'd rather dance with you in the rain

Even on the days when the rain is caused by my
own pain

Especially on those days remind me that once
the clouds clear that's when the rainbow brings
even more color to the sky

Some days I just need reminded come what may
we will be alright

Because the days before you lit up my sky's like
the fourth of July I could always see the horizon
but never felt the beauty deep within

And although I'm not used to having emotions
tell me this is only the beginning and not the end

We'll have so many days together that we've
been dreaming about

Just let me know that's true on the days that I
doubt

Cause even though some days the weather has to
run its course

There's days up ahead that'll be as beautiful as
the day we spent on the dead sea shore

Closure

I don't need cloSure

I know thAt it's over

After so long of avoiding Messy feelings

I nEver thought from you I'd need healing

I thought ouR fate was written in the stars

I wanted you near but for you I'd travel so far

The smile on my face was finally not forced

For you I would've fought in the most gruesome
of emotional wars

When it came to you and I, baby I was all in

I just wanted to be your lover and best friend

I wanted to shout from the rooftops that you
were mine

But you kept me like a secret like I was
something to hide

Telling me you couldn't wait to hold my hand in
the streets

And then take me home and roll around in the
sheets

But when the time came it felt as if affection
became such a burden

Laying right next to you but felt so alone with
no warning

Then switching it up saying PDA wasn't your
thing

Making me feel like you just wanted me to go
away

It's been years since I allowed myself to feel
anything close to how I felt for you

I wore my heart on my sleeve because I thought
what we had was true

You used to say by any means you didn't want to
lose me

But you watched me slip right through your
fingers and left me in a sea of lonely

Even through the distance, every night I longed
for your touch

I was so excited to feel it again but when I did it
felt so rough

Consuming my mind with ways to make you
happy and feel cared for

I just wanted you to see that you were the one I
adored

But the words I said were rarely reciprocated
and fell on deaf ears

After the touch of my fingertips you told me you
needed space, that I was too near

Not at all concerned with just how much I
wanted to be wrapped in your arms at the end of
the day

Excited to see your reaction but I never thought
my hard work you wanted to keep in your
suitcase, the gift that I crocheted

So many nights I dreamt about giving you
everything you wanted

But now when I think of the future you'll just be
a ghost of my past that's haunted

Always in the back of my mind of what could
have been

If only you weren't ashamed, not even wanting
the people you know to know we were friends

And I know I'll eventually stop wondering why

So I'll hold onto the memories of the times we
were happy side by side

I truly hope you get everything in life that you're
looking for

Even if it's not me anymore

Because I know I'll carry on living this life that I
love

Because even if I wasn't for you, I know that I
am enough

I know that if I ever decide to open my heart
again

It won't be to someone who's ashamed to show
we're more than friends

Because I know what I have to offer is beautiful

Even if you couldn't see that that was true

So I know at some point I really won't need
closure

But God damn does it hurt right now, knowing
that it's over

Even Still

I Still wear your t-shirt to bed

You're the one I miss, I cAn't get you out of my head

You wanted the typical family dreaM

But that's not my drEam, I couldn't give you what you need

No matter how beautiful we weRe

I always knew you wanted more

You were looking for a bride

But for that I would never be right

You wanted to have kids of you're own

And all I want is everything this world has to offer and more

So our goodbye was inevitable yet still we tried

But even now I miss you everyday and every night

Because neither one of us could have planned our fates entangling the way they did

Both so infatuated the moment it began

We did our best with the distance between our worlds

And even through the thousands of miles that separated I still felt like your girl

But now those miles are filled with the "I miss yous" that we'll never hear

The 'what could've beens' so loud and clear

So many trips I planned with you in my head

But the ones we had I'll never forget

So whenever you're feeling lonely or sad just
know you're still in my heart

Because you and I, together we were art

So thank you for the beautiful memories I'll
forever hold on to

Just know no matter how much time passes by I
will never forget you

Truth and Dare

I had thiS idea of you

> And the more time went on
> filled with spAce

The More it felt to be true

> It almost fElt real when I would
> dream of your embrace

I could pictuRe your face in my mind

> And almost feel your heart in
> my hands

Even though you were so far away you sure felt
like you were mine

And I imagined our future and
how everything would fall into
place just the way I planned

The person I met so infatuated with who I am

The feelings I felt towards you
were just the same

We seemed to go from zero to sixty the moment
it began

And even after we parted ways
it felt like we were intensified
by fire flame

Over the next six months I held onto that not
knowing my idea of you would cause the fire to
burn out

I know we wanted each other
but I couldn't live up to your
idea of me either

For so long we would comfort each other
whenever we would doubt

You want to settle down and
build a family even though
we knew that idea I've
never been a believer

So we still tried and met up in a country neither
one of us calls home

We talked about moving there
and in the moment reminisced
in that fantasy

I thought during that time you'd sweep me off
my feet with romance but instead I felt so alone

And in your eyes I could see you
realizing the different lives we
wanted and resenting me

But I know we were beautiful once upon a time

Our bodies floating on top of
each other in the dead sea
where we couldn't drown

And we held onto that, crashing into the end of
our fantasy we blindly designed

Nothing left except the beats of
our broken hearts and the
flames that burned us down

But I know I'll hold onto the idea I had of you

Because even if it was never
meant to be

At one point in time it didn't matter that it felt
too good to be true

Those few short months in
fantasy we set each other
free

So when you think back to our moment in time

I hope you remember the
happiness I know we both
shared

Back when I was yours and you were mine

Because even through the
complications of truth we said
fuck it all and took the dare

Home in your Arms

What a time to be alive

Our smiles so Genuine side by side

Getting caught up in the adventuRes we share

Making friEnds with turtles deer racoons and bears

Snorkeling toGether in the bluest springs

Happiness encompassing you and me

It feels so natural spending my days and nights with you

Seeing so many beautiful sights together but
your smile has been my favorite view

The first time you kissed me was as cute as
could be

And since then we've been living out our dreams
in reality

Your cute little thank yous you say after I kiss
you when I'm lost in the moment

Both of us appreciating each other so much
more than just going through the motions

Holding you so tight on the back of your
four-wheeler feels like home

Jumping in your truck onto the next adventure
we go

Camping in the back of your trucking and
waking up by your side to the morning sunrise

Then chasing the sunsets together every night

All our cute little pictures perfectly capturing
our happiness that seems to always be there

There's nowhere I don't want to go with you as
we plan all the adventures we're going to have
everywhere

You truly are such a genuine and happy person

From you there's already been so much I've
learned

So thank you for being exactly who you are

Because I feel at home when I'm wrapped in
your arms

Below the Surface

Beauty In The Pain

My whole life I have never been shy of
expressing my truths in words

But at times they didn't seem enough and I often
yearned for more

I could talk or write till I had nothing left to
articulate

But even then what I was explaining, not
everyone could relate

I know it's not common, the truths that I tell, yet
still they tried

But words only go so far, and I know that's true cause there was still hope in their eyes

The common phrases of 'oh your still young though'

Only seeing my youthful look and never my body below

So although words can help describe my reality

I needed something more like an interpersonal therapy

They say pictures are worth a thousand words

But I hope these will show my truth and elicit emotions that there are no words for

Although the price of surviving takes a toll on me everyday

It can also be true what they say, that there really can be beauty in the pain

Instagram **VS** Reality

There's nothing more I want than to live out my own version of success

And this person I am, the one I'm becoming is the one I've liked the best

I've worked so hard to create a future with endless possibilities

To do everything I want to do and see all the places that are calling me

Everything I've given to be where I am

Never expecting anything to be free or someone
to hold my hand

The countless hours of blood, sweat, tears, and
sanity I've sacrificed

I'd do it all again because my biggest dreams
have become my waking life

.

I realized at a young age the choice to succeed
starts from within

But you can't always control it from beginning
to end

There are some factors that can end up deciding
your fate

And I refuse to wait to start living later in life at
the risk of it quickly becoming too late

For as long as I can remember fear has been my
biggest motivation

And the beauty of this world I have not yet seen
is my most intentional inspiration

I have the job I've always wanted

I've faced my internal demons so I'm no longer
haunted

I've learned how to force my desire to drown out
my anxiety and stress

But throughout all these years there's one thing I
can't control like all the rest

.

I wake up every morning inspired from who I
was the day before

Knowing that in this life I will always continue
to become more

But some days—most days—I'm reminded of
the cruelest reality

Pain is the only feeling I know how to feel due
to a lifetime of its unrelentless grip of brutality

.

There are days I am a shell of a human being

The pains so loud but I don't have enough
energy to scream

Some days breathing seems to be beyond my
capability

Most days I'm imprisoned in an endless torture
with no way to break free

.

The inexorable suffocation I am unable to
control

The endless tests, procedures, and medications,
always ending in medical translations of 'I don't
knows'

I'd be accepting of even a one step forward and
five steps back

But instead, all my diagnosis's progressive is
always the shared fact

.

This reality I've created for myself is everything
I've ever wanted

But most days all I can see is the pain and its
crippling darkness

I love my life and the endless possibilities in my
future

But most days I don't know how to be alive
because it is out of my control that I am the
cause of this perpetual torture

.

Although this reality has forced me to live now
instead of waiting for the false concept of 'when
the time is right'

Ensuring I never put my dreams on hold because
I truly never thought I'd make it past twenty-five

Living out all my dreams now may seem
beautiful on the outside

But to be honest I'd give anything to live a
mundane life

I'd trade it all if it meant chronic pain was not
my main description

And that I was not born from the beginning
unbearably exhausted

So although my reality is everything I want it to
be

Most days I don't even know how to be alive,
and I know this agony, I'll never be able to break
free

Stalemate Dream State

It's often hard to dissect which diagnosis is
controlling my life at any given time

It's more like scribbled chaos constantly
changing its design

The vicious cycles of cause and effect make
never-ending circles not straight lines

The symptoms from one disorder causes a spiral
of another diseases decline

So many nights I lie awake unable to sleep from
the agony of pain in every inch of my body

Digging my nails into my nerves for even the
smallest relief to only cause my skin to rip until
its bloody

Grasping to the five seconds of pressure point
releases like a split second fix for a junkie

Only for the pain to instantly come back worse
than before and smother me

.

Days on end I can't sleep for more than three
hours

Even though that's all I want, the pain takes the
possibility away and so cruelly devours

And the worst part is not getting enough sleep
increases the torture and its unrelenting power

The lack of sleep causes the pain to get louder
and louder

.

The cycle is almost impossible to break

It takes control of my mind and body like an all
consuming plague

I want to sleep but the pain keeps me awake

But the agony gets worse when I don't sleep and
it's always more than I can take

.

This tormenting dance with the devil turns me
into a zombie

Although my Idiopathic Hypersomnia already
causes fatigue and exhaustion so excessively

When the stalemate dream state cycle gets added
to the mix my symptoms increase so
aggressively

I feel myself slip away until I'm trapped in this
cage of torture holding my breath until I can
finally break free

Screaming in Silence

Have you ever felt like you were screaming in silence

Longing for a way to get it out of your head, all this violence

I have, but instead I put on a show with a pretty smile and loud laughter

Because there's nothing anyone can do for an incurable disaster

.

I live it up and chase even the smallest of moments that make me feel alive

Because I don't want my illnesses to be the only
way that I am defined

It's easy to allow others to only see the good

Because explaining the depth of the pain and
suffering can often be misunderstood

.

So instead I've perfected the ability to keep it all
in my head

Because others can't be burdened with my pain
described by words if they are never said

So on days I can bare it I put on a mask and
dress up as pretty as can be

And I highlight moments of smiles and laughter
I have devised so perfectly

.

After all this time I've learned how not to give
into the constraints of an either/or

I've forced myself to enjoy the beauty of every
moment, even though I can never stop the pain
of this internal war

Throughout the years of suffering I've mastered
the art of screaming in silence

Never wanting to project the hopelessness of
battling my debilitating internal violence

.

So I'll hold onto the moments that are louder
than my pain

And never take for granted the illusion of a
rainbow that shines even in the rain

The pain is always there just underneath my
vacant eyes and rehearsed smile

But the moments that are louder than the pain is
what makes surviving worthwhile

Burn Your Pity

Swallow Your Sympathy

We all live in our own realities

We experience our own individual joys and tragedies

We're quick to display our happiness to the world

But hide the smoke every time we crash and burn

We've been conditioned for so long not to burden others when our own life gets too much to bear

Only talk about the rainbow, but the storm is
best not to share

❧

I've never understood how others get to decide
when I'm being too open with the struggles I
can't control

How I should be quieter because my problems
leave no room for hope

Empathy may seem appropriate, but after fifteen
years not even I comprehend my daily fight just
to survive

Every second of my all-consuming pain will
never comfort you with the delusion that
optimism can be intertwined

❧

So understand that your sympathy is offensive in
the most unintentional way

But it is not up for debate whether or not being
offended is or is not okay

Hopeful comments and convincing yourself that
I'll one day get better always seem to follow
sympathy

But with each new diagnosis there never seems
to be any type of remedy

※

Although I've managed to figure out ways to be
stronger than my many diagnosis

Over the years, getting worse day by day, I can't
seem to be tougher than my uncontrollable
weaknesses

And although the toll it takes is far more than I
can handle

Other people's pity does not make me any less
fragile

※

I have fifteen years of proof and daily reminders
that I'm never going to get better

And with each new diagnosis I'm always
informed it's only going to get worse for the rest
of my forever

Doctors have become a part-time job with
endless tests that I always seem to fail

You wouldn't tell a lifetime inmate things will
get better, although I'm not incarcerated I'm still
stuck in my own forced jail

❧

So if you don't know how to respond outside of
sympathy or pity

And knowing about my reality makes you feel
uncomfortable or unsteady

Sometimes I just need to express how
consuming shitty health is especially since the
pain you can't see visibly

But for all our sake burn your pity and swallow
your sympathy

Broken Memories

Childhood & Unicorns & Fairies & Make-believe

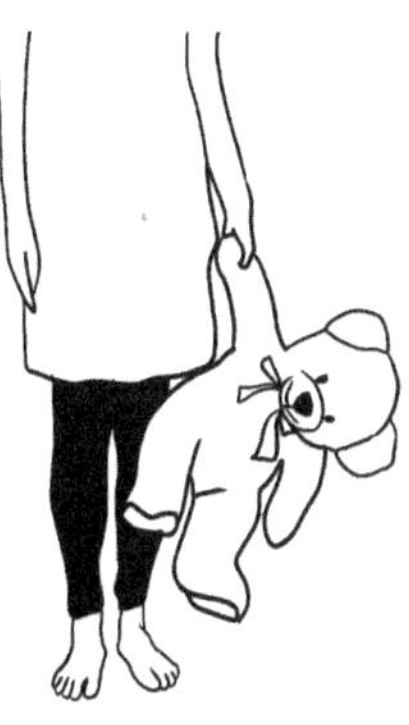

Was I ever actually a child?

Did I ever have an imagination that ran wild?

I can't recall the days when I was young

I've been told I've always had an old soul, maybe
I've just always been numb

I've seen pictures of my younger self

But honestly I feel like I just started existing
when I was twelve

I don't remember birthday parties or the
elementary school days

If I was ever that young, maybe I was just living
in a haze

I've stared at a picture of a moment in time when
I was fishing with my dad

And I try to remember but I feel like the
memories made up the fun that we had

There's proof these moments happened once
upon a time

But I can't see them in my mind, they don't feel
like they're mine

Maybe that's why I have such a young face

Cause the first twelve years, maybe that time
was erased

I don't remember the things my family talks
about

I can't remember the tire swing or summer
outings or going to a friend's house

I've been told about all these things and can
repeat what I've heard

But they're not my memories, all the details I
had to later on learn

I can't remember the moments that shaped who I
was when I finally started existing

So much of what has made me who I am are
parts of me that I feel like I'm missing

Maybe that's why at thirty I'm only four foot
nine

I've always liked my height but maybe I've
always been this size my entire life

I know some people grow up fast but I really
think I just skipped my youth

No memories in my mind, pictures are the only
proof

I'll admit even to me it seems strange

But I've always accepted it because I've always
felt this way

Sometimes I wonder why that part of me is
missing

Only sometimes do I find myself reminiscing

But I have nothing pulling me back to those days

To me childhood is just some made-up magical
phrase

But to be honest how do I know it's something I
should miss

Nothing to hold on to, no one to forgive

There's no way of knowing if I'm better off this
way

Nothing to miss or wish I could change

So maybe I really have always been an old soul

Only knowing my childhood existed because
that's what I've been told

I'D CHOOSE THE BEAR

It starts in elementary school

When boys are mean to you because they like you

It continues in middle school when you can't wear shorts that end before your fingertips

And don't distract the boys by wearing pants with rips

It prolongs in high school when wearing a tank top in ninety-degree weather is flaunting it

And you're the reason boys are chasing it

It doesn't change in college when having a good
time at a bar means you're wanting it

We live in a society that has no problem telling
girls how to protect themselves from men

But don't tell little boys how not to grow up to
be pigs

Guys can walk around barefoot with no shirt at
all

But girls running down the street with sports
bras on make guys stop their car to yell out a
catcall

But if we wore full clothing the guys would have
never felt the need to do something wrong

This society speaks out when there's rape in
other cultures

But turns a blind eye when there's blood on their
own hands, completely ignoring that they too
have raised vultures

When there are young girls next store getting
their innocence stolen by 'good citizen' men

Don't look like trouble and you'll have nothing
to defend

That shirt shows too much, your shorts are too
tight

Pretend to talk on the phone if you're walking
home alone at night

This shirt shows cleavage hopefully you'll be
interviewed by a guy

Don't tell anyone he's the reason you have
nightmares at night

You're standing on the subway cause all the seats
are taken

That means you put yourself in a situation where
a guy will take advantage

They'll rub up on you like they weren't prepared
for the stop

But act like you're dramatic for taking a forward
walk

Here in our society they tell girls to come and
speak up if something happened that was out of
their control

But they tell a lie and it's believed by the cops
while dragging the process on for years and
completely diminish your soul

HAUNTING

I'm a ghost

I've lost all hope

The life has been stolen riGht out of me

I'm sufferIng and I can't hide it anymore so people don't see

I've been silenced, my vOice taken away

Because they believe the lie that you carefully constructed you would say

I'm a dead carcass now, the vulture scraped my skeleton dry

It's my fault, huh? I shouldn't have got drunk
that night

It's my fault, I'm a girl, I should've known that
could happen, right?

I'm dying inside while he moves on with his life

All because I blacked out and he told a lie

His privilege far superior than my own

Even though quite a few times I told him no

Now I can't sleep

Afraid of the terrifying ways this'll haunt me so
deep

Have you ever woken up with tears in your
eyes?

Looking at your demons floating while you feel
their breath on your skin in all-black disguise

These terrors haunt me, that you made sure

Another person's touch will forever be hard to
endure

It's like a tree falling in the forest, people can hear

But you've silenced it and made me live a life of fear

I'm just a girl, how would you feel

If my reality was your mother's, sisters', or daughters' to deal

You fucking broke me, and left me emotionless

Because you could, that night I was so drunk I was motionless

It's not fair that you killed me and moved on with your life

You're walking free while I live with the burden of your crime

Forever haunting me till the day I die

To Each Their Own

There's no thread or needle I could use to make
these open wounds sown

You want this, I want that

He wants another, and she wants facts

To each their own

.

My saving grace is a picture in disguise

Because everyone has their own version of truth
and lies

I want to be someone I can't explain

Because if I don't know, could it really cause me
pain

To each their own

.

I've had so many houses but have never known a
home

You've had one but have always felt alone

So tell me, who's really winning here

Because all I see is someone somewhere,
drinking a beer

with no definition of a home

To each their own

.

I don't know who I am or what I'm capable of

But I know, no matter what I won't stop,
regardless of people, money, or love

So I'll tell you first, if you tell me second,
what're you running from

To each their own

Plucked Before She Bloomed

A rose starts out as just a bud

So small before it shows life, completely
untouched

She takes her time allowing her stems and leaves
to grow

Getting taller and stronger before this world she
comes to know

In this phase the onlookers may admire her with
patience

The rose subconsciously praying she won't fall
prey to someone else's temptations

As she's still trying to understand her purpose
and staying untouched while learning how to
bloom

Always hoping she won't get plucked causing
for the remainder of her life to be afflicted with
gloom

But a flower doesn't get to decide when she gets
handled by the touch of another's fingers

Even if it doesn't die after, the effects will
forever linger

When her petals are plucked and lying so broken
on the ground

The rose can still continue her journey never
knowing the missing parts of herself that are no
longer around

Forever she will be broken, never again whole

Before, she had the promise of beauty and
strength, now who she could've been she will
never know

But when the early petals are plucked away as she continues to grow, from the outside it can still look beautiful

But on the inside she's broken, this world is cruel she so early on came to know

The rose even with missing and half-attached petals will do the only thing she knows to do

She will continue to grow against all odds, even with parts of her missing she will fight and still she will bloom

But as she blooms her brokenness creates thorns all along her stem

To prevent others from causing harm too damaging for her to mend

And even though her petals are still beautiful it's her thorns that reveal her truth from her fragile beginning

The thorns she grew because she was no longer whole, so much of her was missing

Her journey was cursed since the very beginning, her brokenness was consuming

But despite all odds she left her weakness and
desolation behind and never stopped blooming

A Life Inspired

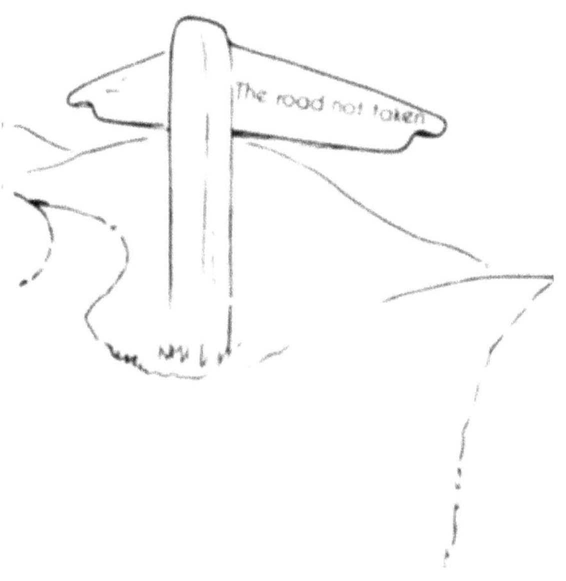

To Travel Is To Live

All the places I've been

It's so true that to travel is to live

I grew up in the southeast of America, Florida will forever be my home

But the more places I've been to the more I want to go

Visited Georgia, Alabama, Tennessee, and the Carolina's

Then lived in Kentucky, even there the beauty of the mountains surprised me

Spending my weekends going to Ohio and Indiana in the search of waterfalls and natural swimming springs

But none compared to everytime I stayed in
Virginia, floating down the Shenandoah river
listening to the bugs and birds sing

One time we lost our car in Maryland coming
back from our visit to New York City

But we still had so much fun, we were just a
couple of gypsies

Going to Washington DC to see all the
monuments

Standing in a place so important, in awe of its
prominence

Then going to Minnesota a few different times

My favorite was when I got to see MGK and
Avril Lavigne live

I spent a year living and exploring so many
beautiful places in Texas

But none compared to the summer I lived in
Colorado that's when I truly experienced the
beauty of the Midwest

Living in Kansas for a month for work but I
made the most of it

I fell in love despite the fact the wind was a
daily struggle, I'll admit

Then spending three days rafting through the
grand canyon was an experience that truly
changed me

I've never felt so small then I did in those days
but beauty was everywhere as far as I could see

Las Vegas was cool with its never-ending
nightlife and the fountain of Bellagio

The music, lights, and water; man what a show

Going to North and South California both so
unique

Each holding its own kind of mystique

But nothing quite compared to the beauty of the
islands of Hawaii

Probably one of my favorite places in the US, I
never wanted to leave

Nineteen states down only thirty-one left to go

I'll see them all that I know for sure

The first time I traveled out of the country was
when I did a semester abroad living in Spain

I was hoping it'd be true that after that I'd never
be the same

The first country I went to was Amsterdam,
what I call the land of the giants who all rode
bikes

Drinking all the water there thinking it'd make
me be alike

Over the six months I spent there I explored all
around Spain

Galicia, Segovia, La Granja, Madrid, Sevilla,
and my favorite Palma Mallorca, so many
beautiful memories etched in my brain

Being in Europe it was so easy to travel so I
didn't stop there

Onto Brussels Belgium where you could smell
the waffles and chocolate in the air

My first experience couch surfing I stayed in a
three-story loft home to seven people

Hopping on a bus and getting off whenever I
decided, stumbling on to so many beautiful
places and cathedrals

Then my first true experience of culture shock
was when I went to Morocco for a few days

It was incredible to see their life lived in such a
different way

The only time I ever missed a flight was when
the metro broke down on my way to the airport
to go spend five days in Paris

So I booked another one because I knew the
memories I'd make there I would always cherish

It was incredible seeing the Eiffel Tower even
though it was under repair

And visiting the catacombs, such a chilling
experience walking down those stairs

Spending a rainy weekend in Portugal was still
one for the books

A different kind of beauty but it was still there if
you looked

Visiting where my ancestors were from in
Ireland was beyond incredible

Not going to lie their accents and kindness were
unforgettable

I always say if I had graduated that semester I
would've never come back, but I know one day
Europe will be my home

So many places left to see and experiences in the
unknown

Our twenty-fifth birthday cruise was the first
time my twin went out of the country

Seven short days but so many beautiful places
we got to see

Every time I travel the most important thing to me is experiencing new cultures and their true way of life

So in Cozumel Mexico we went off the beaten path and learned about their foster homes, it was beautiful how they keep all brothers and sisters together so it can be a little more alright

Then getting to snorkel in the bluest of seas

The underwater beauty is so incredible down in Belize

And our crazy day spent in Mahogany Bay Roatan with the liquor in our veins

It was an experience in itself but I'm glad now we're a little more tame

Experiencing new places with you together

Waiting till we can again because man that was so very special

Last year I spent ten days in Japan exploring so many significant places

Visiting Hiroshima walking through the
heartbreaking memories and the museum, tears
in my eyes and on the pictures of those faces

Seeing how sad history can be

Paying my respect to that tragic memory

In Kyoto walking through the marvelous shrines

Seeing the temples in all their grandeur design

In Nara feeding all the deer in the parks

Even though they bit you when you ran out of
food I still loved it with all my heart

The enigmatic bustle throughout Tokyo was so
alluring

Not a single second in that city was boring

In Japan Mt Fuji is considered a sacred place

Seeing it in person is easy to understand why,
standing over twelve thousand feet tall in all its
beauty and grace

The culture of the past, present, and future is
everywhere you look in Japan

I'll never forget the days spent there inspired
from the second it began

Up next was a place that's always been on my
bucket list

Egypt has always been a place I've been dying to
visit

Landing in Cairo from the first minute the
different way of life didn't take long to see

But it was very apparent even if you don't have a
lot you can still be happy

Riding camels up to the pyramids made
thousands of years ago

So much history there you can hear about but
until you see them you can't even begin to
comprehend the awe until you go

Exploring so many sites on a three-day cruise
down the Nile

During those days time just seemed to stand still
for a while

Stopping in Aswan for horse carriage rides to
the Temple of Edfu

Walking in others' life's work from generations
long before me and you

Final stop in Egypt was Luxor even though we
spent hours at Al Karnak it still wasn't long
enough

I truly think through all the statues there I fell in
love

I took almost three thousand photos all
throughout Egypt during my time exploring

It was so much more than I thought it would be
with each new place even more alluring

After a short flight we landed down in Amman
Jordan

I had no idea the beauty I would see, what a true
fortune

Spending an entire day walking around and
riding a donkey and horses throughout Petra

It was beyond incredible to see the
craftsmanship of that era

Jeep rides and desert campsites in Wadi Rum
were beyond any magical experience I've ever
had

Laying underneath the stars a place I'll always
want to go back

The last day spent floating in the dead sea

Oh the beauty and the memories will now
always be a part of me

My next trip booked is to Peru

I can't wait to explore everything it has to offer
and to spend the day at Machu Picchu

But I won't stop there, I'll never stop exploring

Every place I go creates a new version of me
each one a little less boring

This world is daring with its pushing wind

So I'll travel its path and call it my friend

The Magic Of You And Me

We are made up of star dusts that once belonged
to other galaxies

Inside we hold from other dimensions the roar of
the waves in their seas

Who we are is beyond merely skin and bones

We were made from dynasties in another world
where our beauty lit up their thrones

The light that emits from each one of us will be
the brightest star in the night sky in the distant
future

Our lives started long before our first breath and
won't end in the blink of an eye, that's for sure

The heartbeat that beats so loud with love and
life

Is the same melody that the wind sings on the
wings of butterflies

Inside of our very bodies are the souls from
every friend, stranger, and passerby

From yesterday, our past existence, and every
other life

Our tongues speak words that have been spoken
long before we were here

Every version I was, am, and will ever be,
simultaneously I can feel

I've looked into the eyes I've seen in another life,
past or present we have and will always exist

Our very presence brought on from a shooting
star and someone else's wish

This life is only a page not even a whole chapter

We are living in the unknown constellations both
before and in the life after

Everything that was, is, and will ever be a reality
is coursing through our veins

It may seem impossible but if you think about it
it's really not all that strange

We are not as simple as one single human being

We are magic and that is the beauty of you and
me

Dreams

I have dreams twice the size of me

I'll accomplish them all, you just wait and see

I want to reach for the stars and land on the
moon

And forever be able to sleep in till noon

That sounds like a contradiction, but I assure
you it's not

I'll take a map and travel with a dot

Exploring all the unseen beauty that I dream
about

I want to live a life of poetry, and have nothing
to doubt

Driving the nicest cars in Japan

Then smoking the finest green in Amsterdam

Let's not forget about the trips to the Eiffel
Tower

Dancing under the London lights, drinking
vodka sours

I want to live a life that I create in my dreams

From ball gown beauty queen to a hoodie and
some jeans

This world is daring with its pushing wind

So I'll travel its path and call it my friend

www.ingramcontent.com/pod-product-compliance
Lightning Source LLC
LaVergne TN
LVHW011012200726
843509LV00011B/1066